Gratitude

Stefka Harp

Gratitude
© Stefka Mladenova 2016

National Library of Australia Cataloguing-in-Publication entry

Author: Harp, Stefka, author.

Title: Gratitude / Stefka Harp.

ISBN: 9780992304089 (paperback).

Subjects: Australian poetry — Gratitude — Poetry.

Dewey number: A821.4

Published with the assistance of www.wordwrightediting.com.au

Images courtesy of clker.com and bigstockphotos.com.

www.stefkaharp.com

Contents

Acknowledgements

I wish to express my deep and sincere gratitude to my parents for teaching me the value of life — how to love and be happy as well as show kindness; and to my siblings, for being a part of my life.

My thanks, too, to the Australian Government for opening the door for me to migrate and become a permanent resident; to experience a different kind of life, culture and customs, which has been very enriching, enlightening and eye-opening. I am very grateful for the opportunity I have been given and guided to get to the point I am at.

Sincere gratitude to:

- my daughter for her patience and loving assistance in proofreading my work
- Gail, publishing advisor for the guidance given
- goddaughter Maria, and Dawn, who were willing to read my manuscripts and give constructive comments and feedback.

Dedication

Everything I write and have written so far is dedicated to my family and the divine within, which has guided me through life. At times my ignorance and oblivion to the facts revealed has led to strife and suffering. But these experiences have given me the much-needed fuel for my writings, and I hope they will help others. Life is like a jigsaw puzzle. Some things are meant to happen so that the pieces fit within that puzzle.

S.H.

Disclaimer: The author is expressing beliefs and views based on her life experience. There is no intention to offend anyone who has contrary views. The poems are fun to read and in the process can bring a positive and loving attitude.

Introduction

This set of poems is all to do with gratitude, as the title suggests. It is beneficial to count your blessings every day and give thanks. Just by being grateful for your blessings, the energy released attracts more blessings. The Divine within wants us to be happy, and when you are grateful for something it means you are happy. Therefore the whole universe aligns and opens up to deliver more blessings and happiness to you.

If someone dwells on the negative, the Divine brings more worries to dwell on, thinking that is what it makes the person happy. It is the thought and word energy released by the person that attracts more of the same. Start nullifying the energy created by negative thoughts and words in the past, and stop creating more by becoming aware of your thoughts. Read the poems before bed for a week, and take note of what changes are happening around you.

Isn't it better to dwell on the positive? Even if there is nothing happening, we are benefiting in many ways. Less stress means less tension in the brain, the heart muscle is more relaxed, we tend to be more pleasant and lovable — a delightful person to be around, that's for sure. I know what kind of thoughts I would feed my brain with, and release what kind of energy. Do you?

Stefka Harp

Stefka Harp

Forever I will, with
Obligation to thrill,
Retain faith and free will.

Blessed I am with health,
Enchanted as well,
Infused with love.
Noble soul as pure as a dove,
Gracious life is never dull.

Harmonious to the core,
Always and forever more,
Peaceful nature for sure.
Prosperity comes to the fore,
Yielding happiness galore.

Frankly speaking, with all my heart,
Over and above in delight, I
Refer to the Divine light.

Destined to feel protected,
Indeed hoping to be connected,
Vibrant soul elevated.
If I am to succeed,
Need to do it with speed, very
Eager to plant the seed.

Perfect way to be cultivated,
Rebound and be rejuvenated,
Overwhelmed with love everlasting.
Trust in my core I am grasping, for
Eternal protection I am asking.
Constantly vigilant and on the lookout,
Turning points in life are all about.
Inside of me is a feeling of confidence,
Offset by feelings of competence.
Next: body, mind and soul in congruence.

Fervent I am, and keen to
Obey from here-in
Reunion with the holy within.

To begin with, I ask and pray, a
Habit of mine I have to say,
Every day for me not to stray.

Delicate balancing act is life.
It's a fine line to grind,
Very real I take into account
In the way I go about,
Not for me to know how,
Ensuring I listen to the Divine.

Gladness in my heart forever more,
Understanding the God within for sure.
Intuitative I am, I know,
Dynamic force to acquire,
Appropriately guiding me through the fire.
Negligence is not to coo,
Challenge I have to face and make do,
Effort worth my while to start the day anew.

Fervently I get a grip,
Over the rainbow I leap,
Reunion with the high I seek.

Hassle-free life is
All I want to find,
Vibrant soul to shine
Inside that body of mine.
Noble and free,
Guaranteed to be

Almost an Angel, I agree.

Beyond all question, do not dismiss,
Earthly Angels do exist.
Affectionate and good-willing,
Universal love giving freely,
Today and every day,
Immensely without delay,
Focus on well-wishing sublime,
Utmost kindness and prosperity to find
Lovingly, all the time.

Sacred heart, sanctuary for me,
Overjoyed I am to always give
Unconditional love divine,
Love that makes the soul shine.

Foremost I follow my heart,
Oddly enough with all my might,
Ready to make everything right.

Having all I need to
Accomplish my dreams and succeed
Verifies I have a life,
Indeed makes me come alive.
Nifty way to spend a day without striving,
Gentle and kind nature always thriving.

Aspect to be considered daintily,

Family members addressed gently,
Affectionate love a plenty,
Memory to cherish gladly,
Infinitely as I should.
Lifelong commitment is good,
Yielding eternal happiness forward.

Ferocious my will is to write.
Overnight ideas come with delight,
Radiant thoughts come to light.

Believing in me was
Ever so to be, I
Imagine success,
Neither more nor less, only
Graceful inspiration to access.

Illumination all the way,
Non-stop I crave for
Selection of thoughts I pray.
Prime time for me to acquire
Innermost desire to
Release the power to inspire,
Essential for the soul to aspire,
Devotion to the Divine to transpire.

Timeless treasure to admire,
Occasion to celebrate being aware.

Wonders will never cease, I
Rise and shine at ease.
In the way I know how,
The best of me comes through now,
Effectively, without doubt.

Following my destiny without complaint,
Obsessed I am to maintain or
Rather to invigorate, when

Thinking about my talents.
Hence they are in abundance,
Ever so like garlands.

Tranquillity all around,
All the way to compound,
Leadership within found,
Earthly dreams to be crowned,
Now and forever to rebound,
Time and again to be my playground,
Spontaneously becoming profound.

Inception of the above insight,

Hard and fast like dynamite,
Aiming to re-ignite
Vibrancy within outright,
Eternal body, mind and soul to unite.

Festive and joyful life,
Only way to come alive, I
Rejoice on the count of five.

Hopeful I am, I admit the
Aspect I consider to assist,
Vigorously to exist,
I continue to persist,
Neither turn back nor quit.
Grace upon body and soul I greet.

At long last I am on target,

Living my life within a budget,
Offering a banquet,
Neither more nor less, but adequate,
Glad I am to be as fortunate.

Let it be! Longevity is in view,
I am eager to pursue.
For the love of it, I look into
Eternal life, I believe it is due.

Forgiveness is awesome.
Only brings wisdom to
Restore inner kingdom.

Trust the Divine I do,
Honourable gestures I pursue
Each day and night, it's true.

Warmth within without ado,
Instantly I go and review.
Sagacious I am too,
Destined to have a breakthrough,
Obstacles to look into and
Majestically remove and undo.

Gentleness and love combined would
Attune to the Divine,
Instantly would go and align
Non-stop to define
Eternal wisdom to aspire,
Dignity to transpire.

Focusing on love is a magnet,
Outflow of loving thoughts no limit,
Radiance upon indefinite.

Beaming light ahead of me
Ensuring I do not stray and am free,
Illuminated all the way I aim to be,
New ventures to explore,
Generous outcomes all the more.

Powerful is my habit.
Reassured I reach the target.
Opportunities out there galore.
Simplest way is to know,
Patience to restore,
Elevating my soul Divine.
Revelation would begin,
Omen I am keen,
Undeniably to turn in,
Step closer to prosper.

Faith I have in my heart,
On the look out to assert
Rapid blessings I deserve.

Believing in my birthright,
Ever so grateful and downright,
In pursuit to develop appetite for
Numerous ways by candlelight to have
Grand creations by midnight.

Conceived in the mind,
Revealed by the Divine, to
Enchant and spellbind,
Amazingly to remind.
Troubles being left behind,
Innovation for sure I find,
Vigorously to streamline,
Endless thoughts to finalise.

Fresh start within my domain,
Overflow of hope to maintain
Round the clock to be humane.

Besides other talents I possess,
Emotions I am eager to express.
Intuition as well, I am blessed.
Nonetheless, Divinity I caress.
Goodness! I do it with zest.

Invisible, yet might appear,
Never mind what year,
Today I cheer to make it clear
Universal love and truth I revere.
Instantly I endear,
Thoroughly to be sincere,
Intuition to persevere
Veraciously to a new frontier,
Ever more intuition to hold dear.

Far and wide I yell,
Overflow of wellness to excel, to
Rejoice and feel well.

Tons of goodness in my life,
Happily embracing being alive, an
Electrifying moment to be precise.

Generating energy, I need
Occasion to plant the seed,
Outstanding way to succeed,
Disseminating goodwill indeed.

Inevitable for a good deed,
Now and forever I need to proceed.

Magnificent life to ponder,
Yes, love brings wonder.

Love everlasting is on its way,
Instantly this day.
Follow my heart, I will,
Expecting life to be a thrill.

Frugal I am most of the time.
Overall I never resign, but
Rebound on the count of nine.

Tremendous possibility to
Have all I need,
Endless supplies indeed.

Instant gratitude is due,
Not to be neglected, but reviewed,
Strictly speaking with delight, I
Take it straight to my heart. I
Attune with the Divine,
Nifty way to feel alive and
To have the time of my life.

Although not always clear,
Beyond all I believe and persevere.
Unknown becomes known,
Now I have spiritually grown. I
Do not wait to feel great, yet
Amazingly I always do,
Namely because I am happy too.
Continually I coo for
Everlasting abundance to woo.

Focused on my needs,
Onward I proceed,
Rare event indeed.

The ultimate outcome is abundance
Here to stay in earnest,
Expectation of no less to manifest.

Delicious meals on my plate,
Acceleration of what I expect,
Intending for all that to protect.
Life abundant I treasure,
Yes, in delight and pleasure.

Focusing on the here and now,
Odd it might sound, but I vow
Over and above joyful life to multiply,
Divine gratitude gracefully to glorify.

Far more I suggest an
Ordinary request
Reaching for the best.

Light within abound,
Instant awareness found,
Vigilance to bestow,
Invigorating myself spiritually to grow.
Never too late to explore
Grandeur of life to know

In its entirety, the inner voice is
Nothing else but poise.

Therefore I think and live in the now.
Hesitation is not around.
Enthusiastically I pronounce,

Now is the time.
Overflow of love and loving mind
Well wishing for the world to chime.

Fortunately I have no regrets, for being
Open-minded and proactive
Reassures me I am on target.

Before making loyal friends, I
Endeavour to be loyal in return.
In this way, friendship I display.
No way could I fail,
God willing the friendship will stay.

As I am sure some day

Loyalty will be underway,
Once in a while to convey
Yes, without delay,
At long last without dismay,
Loyal friends I have every day.

For what it is worth in the end,
Reality is spiritually to ascend.
In no time become aware of
Endless love, trust and respect, to aspire
Never to tire, nor
Doubtful I become until I expire.

First of all I ask
Open-heartedly for trust,
Reinforcing faith fast.

Reaching out with respect,
Expecting to connect,
Sprightly to a prayer,
Pleasantly I declare,
Evoking passion to flare.
Confidence to attain,
Today and everyday to maintain.

Safely over the rainbow,
Holiness to know and be aglow,
Onset of humility to overflow.
Wonders will never cease, and
No divine soul will ever displease.

Faithfully I praise and pray,
Obligation I vow without delay,
Ray of hope underway.

Timeless universe always there.
Hooray! There is no scare,
Everyone is in my prayer.

Winsome universe brings astir,
Almost out of nowhere.
Yippee! I jump for joy with flair.

I rejoice in the knowing,

As I have being growing,
Merit being worth exploring.

First and foremost be grateful,
Off you go and be praiseful
Rather than being pitiful.

Beam with love and hope,
Encouraged to gallop
Into the Divine domain, where
No one could inflict pain,
Graceful vigilance to be maintained,

Safe and sound remain.
Approach matters over again,
Fearless attitude to attain
Emotions benefiting heart and brain.

Forever I cheer
Openly, year after year.
Rejuvenation is here.

Blessed I am to be healthy.
Enjoy life I do and I am happy.
Imminent it is for Divine glory
Never to turn back nor worry,
Galloping the path of the holy.

Heart and soul leap for joy.
Every new day is a story.
Alive and abound, at
Long last the best I have found,
Triumphant all the way,
Happily treading as I pray
Yearly rounds, that's the game I play.

Faith I have in my desires,
Once in a while I set them on fire,
Receiving what I require.

Beyond any doubt, what
Each and everyone is about, to
Increase our wealth with time,
Never mind what kind, with
Great imagination of the mind.

With the best of my intentions, I
Envisage wealthy inspirations in
Accord with my thoughts.
Love expressed binds the words.
The desired end is here.
Hallelujah! I cheer,
Yes, sincere and so dear.

For what it is worth,
Offset and go forth to
Reclaim my spiritual growth.

Today is the moment to enjoy.
Hence all the way with glory,
Emerging into being holy.

Passionate, I am in earnest.
Real it is at my best,
Essential to request
Serenity to manifest,
Everlasting peace blessed. I
Nominate my needs and impress,
The ultimate outcome is success.

Motivate myself I do,
Onward only to go through,
Majestically life to renew,
Emerging victorious too.
Now and forever,
Thence loving energy to endeavour.

Frankly speaking, I pray to align
Only with the Divine.
Remarkably when I do, sound mind I find,

Healthy body, healthy mind,
As the saying goes every time.
Valid point I have come to know,
Invisible, it might seem so,
Notably somehow comes to the fore.
Grateful I am for sanity bestowed.

Attention I give to my spiritual growth,

Somehow I get to know how I think.
On the whole, almost in a blink, I
Unite with the fountain of youth in a wink.
Never mind the rest, without
Delay, I concentrate to

Master the wisdom of words.
Intentionally I change my thoughts,
Necessary for sound mind to nourish,
Divine soul in a youthful body to flourish.

Friendly soul I nurture,
Onward into the future
Ready to turn it into virtue.

Hearty friends I have,
Affectionate to the core,
Vibrant and generous,
Invigorating and inspiring,
Nurturing and kind.
Gentle souls like mine.

Loving attitudes, take my word,
Obedient to the Divine in accord,
Yet loyal to themselves
As well as their friends. Ray of
Light upon us, I dare to say.

Fortunate I am to have such friends,
Rejuvenating my soul on end
Indefinitely, for my eternal sustenance.
Empowering and elevating
Night and day, creating a
Delight in expressing gratitude and
Steady flow of positive attitude.

Fearless image I hold,
On and on to uphold
Rightful Divine protection to unfold.

Harmony reigns supreme.
Overjoyed I am, the key to be free
Morning, noon and night,
Emblazoning my home and bright.

Safe and secure I feel.
Warmth radiates to overspill
Every moment I live,
Every moment I forgive,
Thanking the Divine for more to give.

Humble domain infused with love,
Once a day at least I coo like a dove.
My home is divinely protected,
Excellence to the core incorporated.

Free will I have infinitely,
One and only fortunately,
Reward for me definitely.

Having a life for me to embrace,
Alliance with the Divine to caress,
Valuable lesson is to know,
Illumination upon me for sure.
Near and dear is life,
Glorious gift from the Divine.

Alert I am, and clear.

Life is dear.
Its fountain of youth near.
Fair to say I have been blessed,
Evident it is for more to manifest.

Farfetched it might sound,
Once in a while I look around, a
Reminder comes to mind to

Maintain the wisdom of time,
Yearning to be Divine.

First and foremost I pray,
Attention to forgiveness I pay.
Mindful I am of my thoughts,
Innate feelings, I take notes.
Loving gratitude I send out,
Yes, Divine protection I get, no doubt.

Sheer joy to have Divine connection,
Asking for safety and protection.
Frequently as I possibly can do,
Ever the eternal spirit to pursue,
Therefore with time spiritually I grew,
Youthfulness bestowed as new.

From A to Z,
Once in awhile I forget to
Rejoice in life and reflect.

Believing in success, I am
Earnestly doing my best,
Imagination aplenty I confess,
Non-stop I praise and bless,
Goodness in my heart I gladly caress.

So long with reverence, I
Understand the law of the Universe.
Consistent output of loving thoughts
Creates and brings spiritual growth.
Everything I pray for I dwell on,
Success, happiness, health and wealth,
Sure to manifest with a swell, I
Focus on the positive with all my might
Until I feel it in my heart.
Let it be! Success gracefully comes to me.

Faithfully I do reach out.
Overnight the energies rebound,
Ray of hope is all around.

Rise and shine I do,
Every morning anew,
Attribute of mine I say,
Captivating the beauty of the day.
Hoping to reach the world by
Inspiring loving thoughts and words.
Non-stop I bless and request
Goodness in every heart to manifest.

Onset of motion of energies
Unified and carried over in a breeze,
Target to reach at ease.

Faith I have that I exist,
Only way to live and persist,
Rest assured, a fact I never dismiss.

Well and truly I am free,
Happy to be who I am you see,
Obedience to the higher brings harmony.

Innermost feelings tell a story,

A mindset to reach for the holy,
Marvellous way without worry.

About the author

Stefka was born during World War II in a small village tucked away in the foothills of a big mountain in Eastern Macedonia.

Her family, like others in the village, gained their food from the land. It was a self-sufficient household. This lifestyle built much confidence in her and her siblings.

She migrated to Australia in 1972, where she still resides. She finished her degree, and a diploma in counselling, and gained jobs in the welfare sector.

The last seven years before retirement were spent in the DV sector. While working with people she noticed the power of thought in relation to destiny. She believes that when people change their thinking and implement positive and loving thoughts, life changes for better. Prayer, forgiveness, hope and faith go hand in hand with a positive attitude.

Academic achievements

Diploma of Community Services Management

Southbank Institute of TAFE 2006

Diploma in Counselling

Australian Institute of Counsellors 1993–1994

Bachelor of Arts Degree (Major Psychology)

University of Queensland 1989

Economics, book keeping & accounting

Business Studies College (Macedonia)

www.ingramcontent.com/pod-product-compliance
Lightning Source LLC
Chambersburg PA
CBHW071023040426

42443CB00007B/912